THE ADVENTURES OF CAPTAIN CUTTER:
HOW I SAVED THE WORLD

NO MORE BUTTER

Captain Cutter, an ordinary student at the V.V.A. I think not.Cutter is a superhero who loves to eat butter!

However, before this story begins, I think it's important for you to know just where this love of butter comes from. This story goes something like this.

Once upon a time, there was a man named Billy Buttermen. Billy loved butter so much that he opened a butter factory so that everyone could eat more butter. Billy's son, Cutter, is the heir to the Buttermen butter empire, and just like the rest of his family, he loves to eat butter!

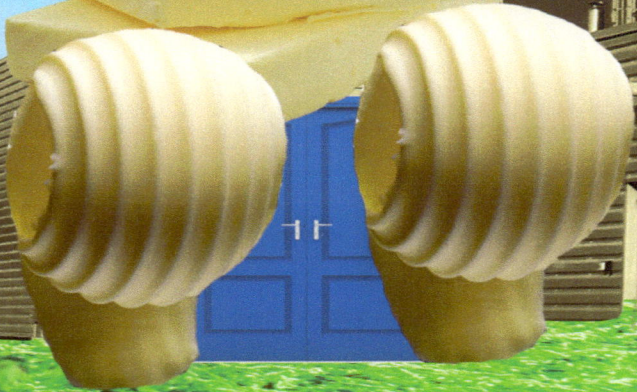

Today is Cutter's first day of school, and that is really where this story begins.

"Lunch is the best part of school," said Cutter as he prepares his school lunch.
"Let's make sure I have everything..."

Butter sandwich
Butter noodles
Icky Licky Moldy Garlic Bread
World Wide Buttery Pie

CUTTER'S LUNCH

Butter Noodles

Butter Sandwich

ICKY LICKY GARLIC BREAD

WORLD WIDE BUTTERY PIE

NO MORE BUTTER

radish

Captain Cutter is eating his favorite lunch when he looks up and sees a huge sign with new cafeteria rules, and the first rule reads NO BUTTER in big, bold red letters. Next, he could not believe when Velga Veggie (Buttermen family's worst enemy) turned off the lights and read all the new cafeteria rules.

"There will be no more butter" shouted Velga and then went on to say. "No more boxed lunches, no more flavored milk, and certainly no more sugar."

All the children were not happy with these rules, especially Cutter, who cannot imagine a world without butter.

After the lights go back on and lunch goes on, Cutter frantically tells his friends. "I can't survive without butter! Simon asks, "Well, what are we going to do?" "Fear not, my friends, because Captain Cutter has a plan.

" Cutter carefully explains, "Velga Veggie has a magical staff that shoots out vegetables, and she calls it the Veggie-O. If we take the staff, she can't make any more vegetables.
" Inspired Simon says, "Then it's set, tomorrow we take the staff."

Today is the day to save the world from the evil Villain Velga Veggie, who is trying to take over the V.V.A.

Cutter and his friends are sitting, discussing their plan while eating their lunch when a new girl named Ava Cada walks by and decides to sit next to them.

"Yesterday, I overhead your plan to steal my mom's staff, so I told her what you were going to do, and she has hidden the staff."

Sitting in the cafeteria feeling very blue, Cutter wonders what he can do, and just when he thinks all hope is lost,
Sugar Cyndi appeared.

"Fear not, Cutter, I know what to do. I can hack into the school computer and change the lunch menu."

Excited and relieved by the news, Cutter and Sugar Cyndi changed the lunch menu.
Butter noodles
Sugar Cookies
Buttermilk
Butter Pie
Butterscotch
Butter popcorn
And garlic bread

All this food sounded so good that Cutter almost fainted!

The very next day at lunch, Velga walks into her office and sees the new lunch menu.
She yells Cutter's name and starts running down the hall like a chicken.
She knows who did this and they will pay.

Mr. Vladimir calls Cutter and Sugar Cyndi to the think-about-it room. With a stern but calm voice, Mr. Vladimir asks, "Children, Mrs. Veggie was very upset today, can you tell me why?"

Cutter quickly yells out, "Mr. Vladimir, I can't live without butter, I just can't!!!" Sugar Cyndi also adds in, "Mrs. Veggie has taken away ALL junk food and BUTTER, so I hacked into her computer and changed the school menu back to the way it used to be."

Mr. Vladimir was shocked and replied, "Sugar Cyndi, you know that was very wrong, and Cutter, no one is asking you to live without butter. I will talk to Mrs. Veggie, but it seems to me that all three of you need a lesson in moderation!"

After Mr. Vladimir talked to everyone, Mrs. Veggie agreed to let some junk food on the school menu. Cutter and Sugar Cyndi apologized for their wrongdoings, and things went back to normal at the V.V.A (Vladimir Vizard Academy).

Mr. Vladimir's lesson for today is: a little bit of moderation goes a really long way!

THINK ABOUT IT

Contributing Authors

WOODSTONE ELEMENTARY
Contributing Authors

Autumn Seltzer

Autumn Seltzer is ten years old. She wants to be an author when she grows up. She is very outgoing and has a huge heart. She is in tumbling, enjoys playing with her little brother, reading and telling wonderful dramatic stories.

Harley Q. Coxson

Harley Q. Coxson is a ten-year-old little girl. She is a super sweet girl who enjoys reading, playing sports, riding horses, and playing outside with friends. Harley wants to work with animals when she grows up.

Allie Dial

Allie Dial is ten years old. She loves spending time with her family, friends, and playing soccer. Allie also has a very creative mind and loves to draw.

Caden Cruz

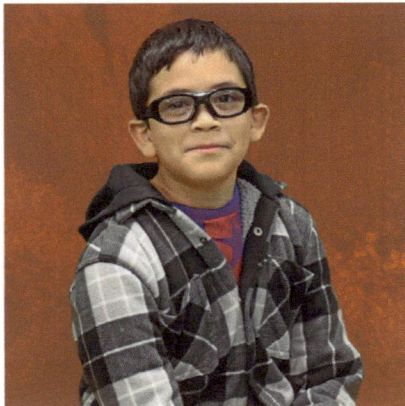

Caden is an eleven-year-old who wants to be an engineer when he grows up. He loves to build and invent things.
In his spare time, he enjoys reading comic books. Caden is a very outgoing and happy boy who likes helping people in any way.

Melody M. Melgoza

Melody M. Melgoza is ten years old and wants to be a veterinarian when she grows up. She enjoys playing basketball, reading books, and caring for animals.

WOODSTONE ELEMENTARY
Contributing Authors

Eliska R. Haenke

Eliska R. Haenke is eleven years old and an aspiring wildlife biologist. She loves the arts just as much as all sciences and is always looking for innovative ways to meld both worlds.

William H.N. Phelps

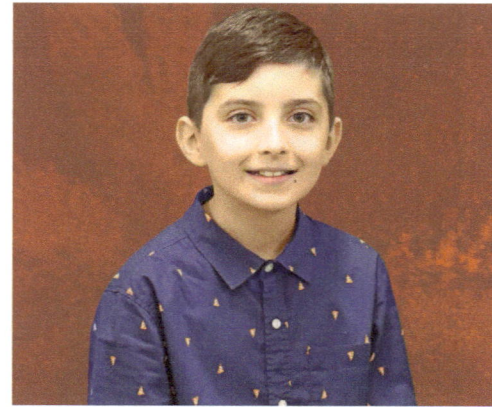

William H.N. Phelps is ten years old, and he wants to be a Zookeeper when he grows up. He likes playing Catan with his family, dancing and playing video games.

WOODSTONE ELEMENTARY
Contributing Authors

Clover C. Brown

Clover C. Brown is eleven years old and wants to be an animator when she grows up. She loves to draw, play video games, build things with Legos and sing. She is in the Gifted and Talented program and enjoys her science and reading classes.

Deyalisa A. Ramos

Deyalisa A. Ramos is ten years old and wants to be a Pastry Chef when she grows up. She loves to read, color, and help others. She enjoys playing with dogs. Dayalisa is a very loving and kind girl; she likes to do what is right at all times. She enjoys playing outside and roller coasters.

Addison Lee Mann

Addison Lee Mann is ten years old and wants to be a fashion designer when she grows up. She loves to create things, dance, volunteer, and sing karaoke. She always puts God before herself, and is loved by many.

Araceli M. Yracheta

Araceli M. Yracheta is ten years old and wants to be a singer when she grows up. She loves to dance in her ballet Folklorico group and loves learning new things. Araceli is an adorable and outgoing girl with a very big heart.

Kaylee R. Bull

Kaylee R. Bull is ten years old and wants to be a writer/illustrator when she grows up. She loves to dance, draw, sing, and help with her little sister. Kaylee is a sweetheart and loves to bring a smile to everyone she meets.

Casper Eller

Casper is an eleven-year-old boy who loves to play video games and would love to design them someday. He has a sweet and helpful nature and loves to go out to movies and restaurants with his family.

Fan Pages

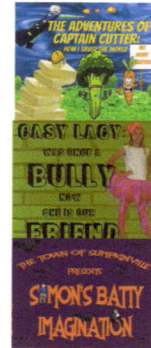

Michael McElroy is eleven years old. He likes to play video games, watch YouTube, and eat hot wings. He plays the piano, trombone, and golf.

MICHAEL MCELROY

SUMPKINVILLE CHARACTERS

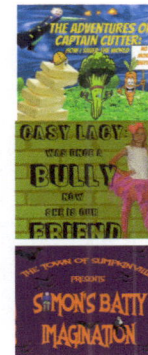

Keane Michael Rhodes is 6 years old and
loves playing football. Keane likes dinosaurs
and wants to be an archeologists when he
grows up. At home, Keane likes to read and
play with his three dogs.

KEANE RHODES

SUMPKINVILLE CHARACTERS

Armani Lillianna Thomas is nine years old and wants to be a singer and dancer when she grows up. She loves to dance, sing, act, and make slime. Armani is very outgoing with a pure heart. She is most definitely girly and eager for what the future holds.

ARMANI LILLIANNA THOMAS

Sean Moore is eleven years old. He is very excited to be in this book. He loves to read and work on computers. He is very outgoing and loves to try new things. When he grows up, he wants to be a doctor or a police officer.

SEAN MOORE

Sumpkinville Characters

Rhyli Eckelberger is six years old. She wants to be a policewoman as soon as she can. Rhyli loves to help others and enjoys helping her mom serve at church. Rhyli loves taking care of her brothers.

Rhyli Eckelberger

Aella R. Merriam is eleven years old and wants to be a ninja when she grows up. She loves to dance and watch Anime. Aella is a sweet girl with a desire to be original and do what is right for her.

Aella R. Merriam

Your Children Our Stories

CSB
INNOVATIONS

www.csbinnovations.com